Potty Training "Mommy & Daddy"

A Guide for Introducing Infant Potty Training As Early As 6 Months Old

MONIQUE SAMUELS

Visit our website at www.notforlazymoms.com.

Library of Congress Control Number: 2020906904

Illustrated by Sayantika Banik

Edited by Sandy Malone

Interior Family Photographs by Regeti Photography and Drew Xeron

Author Biography Photograph by Drew Xeron www.drewxeron.com

Hardback Print ISBN: 978-1-7348395-0-0

Paperback Print ISBN: 978-1-7348395-1-7

EBook ISBN: 978-1-7348395-2-4

*Dedicated to my husband Chris and our beautiful children,
Christopher, II, Milani, and Chase.*

Table of Contents

Welcome to parenthood! You've experienced it all. From sleepless nights, gassy tummies, fevers, colicky cries, embarrassing public outbursts, diaper blowouts, diaper rashes, growth spurts to terrible twos, and more. However, one of the most challenging and frustrating moments every mom and dad will face, usually after the first couple years of being a new parent, is when they find themselves asking the question, "How do I potty train this little human? Why is it that some children catch on earlier than others? What am I doing wrong?"

There are so many cute books on the market that include colorful pictures for children to look at their favorite cartoon characters learning how to use the potty. Why are these books targeting children who cannot read? If kids are visual learners who, like sponges, soak up everything they see and hear from the time they are born, aren't we starting potty training too late? How old is too old before a child becomes set in their ways? They spend the first two years of their lives being brainwashed and encouraged that it's okay to mess themselves. After much time has passed, we then tell them, "Oh no! That's nasty! Don't pee and poo on yourself. Do it on the potty! Where would you get such an idea that messing yourself is okay?"

Do you see the confusion a young child must go through? We help them develop this terrible habit at first. Then later, we expect them to, all of a sudden, turn it off like a light switch just because we feel that they're too big to mess themselves. Babies are much smarter than we give them credit for, and they love a consistent routine! They want to feel secure and they love knowing beforehand what's going to happen throughout their day.

What I learned through my process of self-discovery with my own children was that it's not the baby who needs retraining. It's Mommy and Daddy who need to be trained properly from the beginning. Taking the right approach from the start will save you from having to help your baby unlearn the habits that being in diapers has taught them.

So here we are, finally, with a step-by-step guide that will focus on training Mommy and Daddy on how to approach potty training at a very early age. The following approach is what I like to call the "Monique Method," which is actually an introduction to the potty.

I learned so much having three children who were so different in their ways and who learned to use the potty at different ages. The most important lesson that I learned was that the sooner I introduced using the potty, the less likely they were to fear using the toilet altogether. They knew exactly what the potty was for without having to sit there for hours. And, most importantly, they were fully potty trained faster than most of their peers. Often, we are the roadblock between the diaper and the toilet. It's normal for parents to do what is convenient for them, while also placing limitations on our young ones, due to their age or what we feel is the social norm.

Introduction

Years ago, before I was ever married with kids, I met a woman who was originally born outside of the United States. We had an interesting conversation about children and the differences between how kids in her country were raised versus kids in the United States.

"Take potty training, for instance," she said in her beautiful accent. "We begin potty training in our country as soon as the baby can sit up and is on solid food!"

I was in disbelief and totally confused, but I knew when I had kids, I had to try it. And it worked! Everyone thought I was a crazy first-time mom who was putting too much pressure on my baby. The look of disbelief on their faces as they witnessed my 6-month-old son Christopher communicate to me in his way that he needed to go to the bathroom - and then actually use the potty - was priceless!

When you think about it, babies never like to sit in a mess, which is why they fuss when they need a diaper change. And it's also probably the reason why, even as infants, many will relieve themselves as soon as you remove the diaper during a change. My oldest two babies, Christopher and Milani, were around six months old when I began their potty training journeys. My youngest son, Chase, actually began training when he was 4.5 months old!

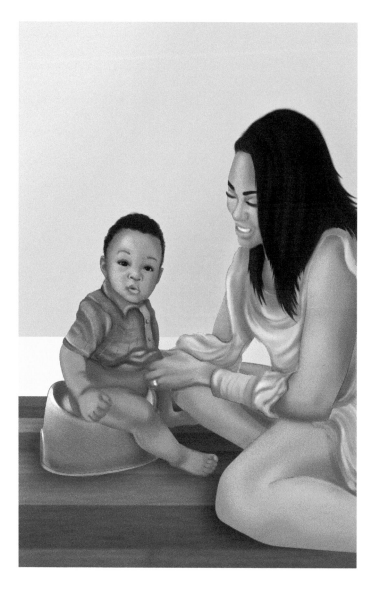

6 month old Christopher & Mommy

Chase was super strong and started sitting up on his own a lot sooner than the other two, and there were other factors that motivated me that are explained later in this guide. But all three of my children began giving me signals of when they had to use the potty within two weeks or less of me starting their training!

The key to their success was for me, my husband, and any other caretakers to be on the same page, be consistent, watch for cues, and establish a routine. The results were clear! Christopher was fully potty trained at 1.5 years old and Milani was exactly one year old. And Chase, who is 19 months old as I write this, is still a work-in-progress. He wears underwear and is diaper free during the day and wears a diaper throughout the night while he sleeps.

I knew Chase was ready when he came to me and started fussing and pulling my pants. I asked him if he had to go to the potty, and he immediately stopped fussing. I grabbed his hand and we walked to the bathroom, and then he proceeded to handle his business after I placed him on the toilet! The process is a little different when you're dealing with a walker, and you'll learn more about that in Step 10 of this guide. But that? Having Chase tell me he needed the potty was definitely a "proud mommy" moment for me.

That was also the green light to transition him completely from pull-ups to big boy briefs!

Step 1: Purchase a travel potty seat

Where do you start? Buy a potty seat, or two.

There are tons of very cute potty seats on the market but I chose to be simple and efficient. A travel potty seat was the best option for me since I am always on the go, and the smallest size was more comfortable for the baby to sit in.

I could easily carry the small seat from room to room. If I had to leave the house, I would pack it in the car, along with some disinfecting wipes and a bottle of water for cleaning the potty after use. There were times when I was on the go with my baby that I would have to find a safe place to park my car, remove my child from his car seat, and set up a bathroom right in the backseat of my car! Always be sure to lock your doors if you're traveling alone. And always be aware of your surroundings and use good judgment! If you're frequently on-the-go or have more than one tiny child, you might consider keeping an extra potty seat in your trunk all the time with a cleanup kit to save yourself time getting out the front door.

As my babies got bigger, I purchased a toilet seat insert that sits directly on the toilet and helps keep the baby from falling into the bowl. Never leave smaller babies unattended on the actual toilet as you don't want the child to fall face-first onto the floor! I always keep flushable wipes near the toilet tissue, so I never have to turn my back at my little ones. With that said, be careful flushing "baby wipes" as many plumbing experts and local sewer authorities advise against it.

Step 2: Be Prepared

When you think you're ready to start potty training, you need to prepare the areas where you're going to use your associated supplies. Having to run and get something during this part of the process is a hot mess and makes it all far more stressful for you and your baby.

As soon as my kids were able to sit up on their own and began eating solid foods, I started their potty training journeys. When Christopher was 6 months old, and I was a first-time mom, everyone around me thought I was either crazy or totally clueless!

Remember, it is not a race. It's important to remember that all kids learn differently and have different methods of communicating. My eldest son caught on to potty training in two weeks, while my daughter took an entire month. My youngest son, Chase, caught on right away but wasn't as consistent in the beginning as his siblings had been.

I learned fast that I had to come up with a way to make the transition from diaper removal to potty rather quickly or risk a real mess. I always removed the diaper and replaced it with a cloth diaper shortly before I expected (or hoped) they would need to relieve themselves. I gently wrapped the cloth diaper around my babies before their feeding sessions since all of my kids had their big poops within minutes of finishing their meals and bottle. Having switched to a loosely wrapped cloth diaper would make the transition to the potty much faster and easier when the time came.

You'll figure out your baby's routine after you use the next step in this guide, and then you can stash your supplies in the appropriate locations. Be sure that the potty and wipes are handy and ready for use, even if that means bringing your potty training kit into the kitchen.

It took some time for me and my baby to get used to this routine. But the better prepared I was in advance, the easier it was for me to catch the baby just before the action began.

Step 3: Tracking Time

The morning is the best time of day to begin your potty training journey. After the baby has enjoyed breakfast, keep track of how long it takes between finishing the meal and making the first bowel movement. I would keep a notepad handy to jot down the time I started the feeding and then the time of the first poop. All of my kids pooped in a 10-15 minute window of time after I fed them. The first few days require a lot of work. Do not be discouraged if you miss an opportunity! I usually start by tracking the "poops" because they don't happen as often as the "pees." They're also much easier to read due to the facial expressions and grunts. You can continue tracking throughout the day and after several days, a pattern will begin to emerge.

Today's Date: _____

Potty Time	Poop/Pee/Both	Diaper Status	Signal Given/Routine Potty Break
10:25am	Poop	Wet	Grunts and facial expression
12:00pm	Both	Dry	Routine Break before nap

Sample Tracking Chart

Step 4: Watch For the Cues

6 month old Christopher & Mommy

We all know the funny faces or the grunts babies make when they're about to poop! As soon as you recognize the smallest sign of this, gently take the diaper or cloth off of the baby (don't scare the baby!) and place them on the potty. Distract the baby by asking questions with excitement, such as, "Do you have to go poo-poo on the potty?" Be sure to brace the baby the entire time so he doesn't fall to either side. At this age, with a smaller potty, the baby should be able to plant their feet on the floor or surface to help hold themselves up.

Some babies give great bowel movement cues by turning red, getting stick stiff, or widening their eyes. You will be surprised at how much this potty training journey forces you to really pay close attention to your baby. Get ready to know your baby on an even deeper, smellier level! If your baby is very inconsistent with their poops or seems to be struggling more than normal, you may want to consult your doctor and consider a daily probiotic suitable for the child's age.

The key here, especially for the first-timers, is to place the baby on the potty almost at the same time as they are about to relieve themselves. You don't want to have your baby sitting on the potty for minutes at a time. Even two whole minutes is too long. The quicker the transition, the better. It took me a few mornings to nail this! Sometimes I would place him on the potty seat too soon, and then he would go as soon as I put the diaper back on. Other times, I was too late and I would just miss the opportunity. Don't give up and do not be discouraged! Consistency is key and you will get the hang of this.

Step 5: Praise! Praise! And More Praise!

After your baby finally finds success and poops in the potty, which shouldn't take more than a minute, go CRAZY with enthusiasm! Give your baby lots of praise and even make up a potty song emphasizing the "P" sound. My eldest son eventually started saying the "P" sound over and over to let me know when he had to go.

If you have older children, invite them to participate in cheering the baby on. Make it a family affair and celebrate the successes together. We have our own Samuels Family celebratory potty song that we've used for years. Now, Christopher and Milani sing it for Chase. Feel free to personalize it or make up your own.

We clap as we sing:

"You go poo poooooo on the potty."

"You go poo poooooo on the potty."

"You go poo poooooo on the potty."

"You go poo poo-poo on the potty, YAY!!!"

We would clap together, and he would have the biggest smile on his face. All your baby wants to do is make Mommy and Daddy happy. The baby may not realize the magnitude of what they've accomplished, but they are happy that Mommy and Daddy have big smiles on their faces and they feel more comfortable because they are not sitting in poop.

I also noticed that singing this song every time I put the baby on the toilet seat, it created a trigger for the baby. As they grew older, sometimes even when they knew they had to go, they would fuss or try to wiggle off the potty. But if I began to sing the potty song, the baby calmed down and usually remembered why they were sitting there and took care of business.

Never make your baby sit on the potty for a long time — more than a couple of minutes is too much. Then clean your baby up and give them plenty of hugs and kisses. This is just the beginning of a successful potty training journey.

Step 6: Different Baby, Different Response

My eldest son gave great cues from the time he was 6.5 months old. He loved the potty song I had created for him and would try to sing along in his own way. He really enjoyed not having to sit in his poop and actually preferred to use the potty.

Christopher began communicating his bathroom needs to me by saying the letter "P" sound over and over. The first time he did this, I thought I was just imagining things. I asked myself, "Could my baby really be making this sound because he has to poop?" Although it wasn't his usual time for a poop session, I decided to make him sit on it just in case. As soon as he sat on the potty, he released it! I was in complete shock! My two weeks of "poopy stalking" had really paid off. Sometimes I missed his cues, and sometimes he didn't give me any.

Either way, I called it a success when he went a full three months without a poopy diaper. As I stated before, tracking pees is much harder than tracking poops so choose your battles wisely. My oldest child's biggest achievement was to learn what the potty was for before his first birthday. He completely understood and never feared using the toilet.

Christopher

My daughter, on the other hand, never gave cues. Instead, she anticipated the potty schedule. It was like clockwork with her! Ten to 15 minutes after she ate, I would put her on the potty seat and she went immediately! She just never communicated that she had to go. Instead, she would wait on me based on her feeding schedule.

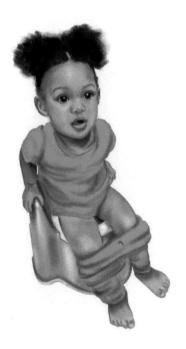

Milani

If I waited too long, she relieved herself in her diaper. I assumed she would potty train just like my son, but I quickly learned she was very, very different from Christopher.

Milani was all about her routine, and if you didn't keep up with her schedule, she did what she had to do, no matter the circumstances. This took some getting used to because I was accustomed to the way Christopher had adapted to my schedule. I quickly realized I had to change my mindset if I wanted her early potty training to be successful. Amazingly, by the time Milani was 10 months old, she was not only using the potty on a consistent basis, but she was also waking up from naps with a dry diaper. She graduated to pull-ups and then the tiniest little girl underwear I had ever seen in my life! She was fully potty trained, including sleeping through the night without a diaper, before she was a year old. Accidents were expected – and they happened occasionally – but her understanding of using the potty at such a young age was pretty incredible.

Lastly, let's talk about my work-in-progress as I write this - my youngest son, Chase. Chase was such a robust and healthy baby. He began sitting up on his own at four months old, but two weeks after that, he underwent a surgery for hernia repair. When I brought him home from the hospital, I was really nervous that he would contaminate his stitches with poop, so I decided to try the potty and see if I could catch him before the action began. I was successful right away and he seemed to quickly realize, "Hey, I don't have to sit in this mess!" He became a consistent little potty pooper.

That lasted until Chase turned a year old and the stubbornness (that he obviously inherited from Daddy) started to kick in. Suddenly, he decided he no longer liked to sit on the potty.

Chase

What had previously been an easy potty time ritual for both of us became something to dread because I could count on my littlest child to throw a fit much of the time.

I'd put him on the potty and he would fuss. I'd say to myself, "well, he hasn't pooped yet, and I'm sure he has to go," and sit with him for just another minute.

But I've never believed in forcing the potty sit-down, so after that minute, I would assume Chase was making a fuss because he didn't need to use it. Then, as soon as I took him off the potty and pulled up his pull-up, he would poop in it! After it happened a few times, I began experimenting with different potty seats and it turned out that had been the problem. Once I understood his potty comfort preferences, we were good to go again.

It's all about trial and error. The important key is to never give up and stay patient with your child. Until they learn to talk, communication can be challenging. Now Chase alternates between coming to get me when he has to go, giving me facial cues, and occasionally having accidents. He is more determined to avoid accidents altogether now that he's transitioned from pull-ups to big boy briefs during the day. I'm most proud that he knows what the potty is for, and that he's not afraid to use it.

This step is probably the most important to remember if you have more than one child. Every baby is uniquely different, including the manner in which they become potty trained. Your baby will teach you in their own particular communication style. No baby is exactly like any other baby. I learned that after having my second child. I had assumed that since Christopher gave me cues and caught on fast, my other babies would do the same thing. Bad assumption. My second and third babies caught on to the potty system, but it took me more time to adapt and learn their unique style. Never compare your child's progress to another child's progress. Your baby will let you know when they're ready to be fully trained.

At the end of the day, it has to make sense to your baby. Be consistent because the day that it finally clicks in their mind, there's no turning back!

Step 7: Potty Breaks

After you have tracked how soon your baby goes to the bathroom after meals and you've had a few successful trips to the potty, you can start timing the potty breaks and create a schedule. Once my babies got the hang of it, I would automatically put them on the potty as soon as they woke up in the morning, after they ate full meals, before naps, and as soon as they woke up from naps. This pattern helps the baby to understand there will be several chances throughout the day to use the potty, and in my experience, they'll be less likely to poop or wet themselves.

I think the worst thing you can do is put your baby on the potty and make them sit there until they go. That feels like punishment to the child, especially if they don't have to go. By starting early, you're training your baby to know that the only time they have to sit on the potty is when they do actually need to use it. Routines are not always easy to stick to, especially if you're traveling or if you have outside caretakers for your child. The crucial part of early potty training is creating a routine that you can stick to, at least during the beginning phases. I created a daily schedule for my kids and posted it in several places throughout my home. This helped me, my husband, our babysitter, and even the daycare stick to the same potty training schedule.

Step 8: Consistency is Key

Once again, I remind you that this guide is not intended to be a drill or a test, but rather an opportunity to introduce the potty very early on. One of the biggest takeaways from this should be that in order to be successful in potty training, you must be as consistent as possible. And even consistency will vary based on the individual child and your family's circumstances when it's time to start potty training.

My oldest son went to daycare off and on throughout his first two years. While I provided schedules and believe his caretakers did their best, his schedule wasn't the same on days he went to daycare as it was when he was at home with me. As a result, he had moments when he would have accidents because of that inconsistency. It didn't stop him from understanding the purpose of the potty and becoming potty trained very early, but it did make things a little more difficult.

I stayed home after my daughter was born and she didn't start pre-school until she was two years old, so I was able to be very consistent with her potty training schedule. Milani was fully potty trained by her first birthday. She did not wet herself during the day, at nap time, or even overnight. She occasionally had accidents when we traveled and her schedule was thrown off, but other than that, my daughter was great about using the potty.

Most of the time when my children have had accidents, it was because there was an interruption in their routine or I simply wasn't paying enough attention. Potty training while you're traveling is even harder than doing it at home because of changes to their surroundings and time zones. But as hard as it is, it's important to do your best to keep up the consistent routine your baby is used to.

Keep in mind that early potty training does not mean you should wait for your child to tell you every time they have to use the potty. Even with my kids now, at ages 7, 5, and 1, I have to tell them to "try" to potty when they tell me, "I don't have to go." I insist they go and most times, they needed to! You never want to allow your child to get into the habit of holding their bladder or their bowels. Continue to encourage bathroom trips on a schedule and never rely on young children to be fully in charge of their bladders.

Step 9: Set Realistic Goals

Set goals for yourself and your baby that you think you can actually achieve. Those goals are not the same for everyone. This process shouldn't be a stressful one for you or your baby. Babies love to please their parents, so the exchange of excitement should be an achievement in itself. I began this journey with my goal to simply capture the poops. They're easier to track and happen less often. If your baby is still wetting, it's okay! Sooner or later, they will get the hang of it. When they're younger in age, it's nearly impossible to capture both the poops and the pees, so be sure to set realistic goals to avoid setting yourself up for disappointment.

Be fully aware of what comes along with early potty training. Once you begin this journey and your child catches on, you will have to maintain the routine. You never want your child to hold their bladder for too long.

Put together a travel potty training kit for yourself so that if you're outside of the home with your child and they need to "go," you are prepared to either set up shop in your car or safely use a public restroom. There are great toilet seat covers on the market that you can purchase to ensure your child doesn't get exposed to germs. I always carry sanitizing wipes or spray with me. And I have repeated the words, "No touching! No touching!" so many times to them while I'm lining the toilet seat that at one point, my kids started saying it to me as soon as we walked into a public restroom.

The truth is some parents simply aren't ready to potty train their kids, and that's totally okay. We all have the freedom to choose how we parent our kids, and as always, this is a judgment-free zone.

I remember the first time I heard another mom explain that she just couldn't start potty training yet. I had taken my then 2-year-old daughter Milani to the bathroom inside an airport. As we were walking out of the stall, a woman with a little girl around the same age as Milani looked at us in shock. She asked how old my daughter was, and then said she couldn't believe she was fully potty trained! She looked relieved as she explained to me, "My daughter is slightly older, but I'm so glad she's still in diapers. It's so much more convenient, especially when traveling!" Early potty training is not for everyone. Just remember that no matter what age you start, you have to set realistic goals to avoid making your child (or yourself) feel overwhelmed or frustrated.

Step 10: Tips and Tricks For Potty Training Walkers

1 year old Christopher & Mommy

The tips in this section will work for you whether you've been working the steps since your child was a baby or you're just starting the potty training journey altogether with a toddler. It may be faster for a child who is already familiar with the potty, but remember that I've warned you not to compare your child to any other child, even your own.

One of my girlfriends started potty training her daughter just as she was approaching her third birthday and they were struggling, so she came to me for help. The biggest difference between starting your potty training journey with a toddler versus a baby is that many toddlers have the ability to speak their minds and, in most cases, think they know it all. The "Terrible Twos" will come sooner than you expected and they can be more challenging than what you've seen in the movies.

For starting first-time potty training with a walker, or transitioning in-progress potty training from baby to toddler, you just start right here with the following tips and tricks:

Tip # 1: Switch to cloth underwear

I remember when I purchased my oldest son's first big kid underwear. Christopher was so excited to wear underpants like a big boy! Talking up the "big kid underwear" is a great way to mentally transition your child for the next step and get them excited. The great thing about wearing cloth underwear is that your child can actually feel when they have an accident. The moment they say, "Uh oh mommy," you know they are ready to be fully potty trained.

As with newborns, most walkers do not like feeling wet and messy. Unlike cloth diapers, disposable diapers and pull-ups are absorbent and designed specifically so that your child doesn't fully feel the mess they make on themselves. When you allow your children to actually feel that they wet themselves (while at the home, of course), it triggers something in their minds (most of the time) that something isn't right. Toddlers realize that there must be a better way! Letting them feel that uncomfortable feeling gives you a chance to encourage and reinforce potty use. Consistency, repetition, and encouragement are crucial.

I told my girlfriend who was starting the potty training journey with her 3 year old to switch to cloth underwear and wait and see if her daughter reacted with shock when she wet herself and felt the discomfort from the wetness. If she alerts Mommy that there's a problem, she's ready for training. The toddler acknowledging their accident is giving you clues that they are ready to potty train! If the child totally ignores the wetness they are feeling, they're probably not quite ready to be trained and may need more time.

Fortunately for my girlfriend, her daughter picked up on it quickly and they found success!

Super Hero Milani

Tip # 2: Prepare to clean up a daytime mess

One of the best ways to help prepare your toddler for big kid underwear is to let them roam around your house without any pants at all for part of each day. During this time, it may feel more like you're housebreaking a puppy than potty training a kid, but that's okay.

When Chase became an official walker, I started this "puppy mode" process with him. One day I was in the kitchen and Chase walked over to me diaper free and began to relieve himself on my floor! I didn't get upset because I appreciated the fact that he stopped what he was doing, found me, and in his way, let me know that he needed to go. I immediately picked him up and ran to the bathroom as I encouraged him to go on the potty. Eventually, it will click. It did for my two older children and it has worked for my friends who have tried this strategy with their toddlers.

Next, we tried the same thing with Chase wearing big boy underpants. Sitting in wet cotton underwear isn't comfortable, and he quickly learned to alert me if he needed the potty. Sometimes he told me right after he had messed himself. But that was okay because it showed he was learning. If he had been wearing a diaper or pull-up instead of his big kid cotton underwear, he would have continued to play without alerting me. The simple fact that he would come to let me know he had made a mess was progress.

Every step achieved is a move in the right direction. Set aside some time each day to try "puppy mode" and you may notice a huge difference in your child's potty behavior. Remember to frequently ask your child if they have to go potty to cut down your cleanup time when they're going commando. Although it can be frustrating and messy, I try to find the positives in every situation and the effort I made when the kids were in "puppy mode" was really well worth it.

Tip # 3: Take potty training your toddler in stages

Everything happens one step at a time. After your child has mastered wearing big kid underwear in your home, the next step is to test their success with it when you're on the go. Start by letting your child wear big kid underwear when you take them with you to run a quick errand or two. Pack at least two changes of clothing, and two extra pairs of underpants, because accidents will happen. As I said before, I always keep a travel potty, baby wipes, and sanitizer in my car just in case we need it. The worst thing that you can do while you're potty training is force your child to hold their bladder, so the key is to always be prepared. Once you and your child have been successful on quick trips out of the house in big kid underwear, you can be brave and try it for longer adventures.

Tip # 4: Establish a cutoff time for juice or other sugary drinks.

Studies have shown that sugary beverages will trigger your urge to urinate more often, so the odds of overnight accidents greatly decrease when you establish a cutoff time for juice for your child. My children go to bed at 8 p.m., so after 6 p.m., I only offer them water to drink if they are thirsty. I never discourage my kids from drinking if they feel thirsty; but rather, I simply make sure they're drinking water so they can have a longer period of uninterrupted sleep.

Tip # 5: Bedtime potty break

In our home, we have made using the potty right before bed a pretty consistent ritual. Remembering to make one final opportunity for the kids to use the potty before they go to bed will lessen the likelihood of an accident during the night. Unfortunately, bedtime routines can get overwhelming, especially if you have multiple children with a variety of different end-of-day and tuck-in needs. But regardless of what distractions happen between putting on the jammies and actually saying goodnight, making one last trip to the potty should be a priority before you tuck your little one in for the night.

Tip # 6: Prepare to clean up a nighttime mess.

Invest in a machine-washable mattress protector before you start overnight potty training. For the first few days of overnight training with each of my children, I washed bed sheets every morning, and sometimes in the middle of the night.

It's okay to pause your progress if your child doesn't seem quite ready – we did. I simply put the overnight pull-up back on and decided to try again later. Then, after a few mornings of waking up with dry overnight pull-ups, I gave it another shot. I could have cried tears of joy the first time my child woke up on their own and alerted me that they had to go potty!

Conclusion

Christopher, Milani and Chase

You'll be surprised at how the potty training journey will also help you learn more about your baby's health and overall attitude. For example, I always knew when my infant son was getting sick because he would poop on himself while he slept. From the time he was six months old and we started potty training, Christopher didn't poop in his sleep. In fact, I remember being surprised to learn from other moms that their kids regularly pooped in their diapers while they were sleeping.

Since my son had been introduced to the potty early and I knew this about him, I knew that if he pooped in his sleep he was probably coming down with something and hadn't been able to hold his bowels. Having this knowledge allowed me to get a head start on remedying him using my natural methods and/or taking a trip to the doctor's office. As a result, Christopher usually avoided the bug or wouldn't be sick as long as he would have been had I not found out he wasn't feeling well until a few days later.

Also, beware of the regression your child may experience. Sometimes, even after your child is fully potty trained, there may be situations that will cause them to regress and have accidents. Major life changes like moving, starting a new school or daycare, having a new sibling, or suffering a tragedy, God forbid, can cause your child to revert back to their old ways.

When my daughter was born, my first child, Christopher, was 2.5 years old and had been pretty well potty trained for some time. But then, after we brought Milani home from the hospital, Christopher randomly began having more accidents than usual. We thought it might be because he saw the new baby wearing diapers and getting lots of attention, that maybe he wanted to be the baby again. Our pediatrician confirmed that this was very normal and said to keep encouraging Christopher to use the potty like a big boy.

Christopher had been potty trained for so long at that point that we were no longer giving him the praise we once did for using the potty. It felt unnecessary. But after he had to share our attention with his new sibling, we realized that we had to make sure Christopher received praise for doing even small things. He needed even more praise when he hadn't had any accidents for a while in order to encourage him out of this regressed behavior. After two weeks, he was back to normal! Milani, on the other hand, did not have any potty training regression issues when Chase was born. As I stated before, every child is different!

There are so many lessons like this that baby can teach Mommy and Daddy simply by potty training early! You know your baby on the outside, but potty training takes you to a whole new depth of understanding.

The confidence I witnessed in each of my children was truly amazing.

Always remember that every child is different and may require you to try different techniques. It's your job to figure out which ones work best for your child. The primary goal of this guide is to INTRODUCE the potty to your baby at an earlier age. We're not looking for perfection as much as we are looking for familiarity. When your child realizes that they don't have to sit in a mess, you'll be surprised at how quickly they catch on. Using these techniques explained in the 10 steps I've outlined, all three of my children adjusted to their potty routine quickly, never had a fear of the potty, were fully potty trained faster than their peers, and understood clearly that the potty was not for playtime.

Your baby is ready for potty training anytime you are. And after reading this step-by-step guide, Mommy and

Daddy are finally ready for potty training, too. Good luck with your potty training journey!

Tracking Chart

DATE: _____

Potty Time	Poop/Pee/Both	Diaper Status	Signal Given/Routine Potty Break

DATE: _____

Potty Time	Poop/Pee/Both	Diaper Status	Signal Given/Routine Potty Break

DATE: _____

Potty Time	Poop/Pee/Both	Diaper Status	Signal Given/Routine Potty Break

DATE: _____

Potty Time	Poop/Pee/Both	Diaper Status	Signal Given/Routine Potty Break

DATE: _____

Potty Time	Poop/Pee/Both	Diaper Status	Signal Given/Routine Potty Break

DATE: _____

Potty Time	Poop/Pee/Both	Diaper Status	Signal Given/Routine Potty Break

DATE: _____

Potty Time	Poop/Pee/Both	Diaper Status	Signal Given/Routine Potty Break

DATE: _____

Potty Time	Poop/Pee/Both	Diaper Status	Signal Given/Routine Potty Break

DATE: _____

Potty Time	Poop/Pee/Both	Diaper Status	Signal Given/Routine Potty Break

DATE: _____

Potty Time	Poop/Pee/Both	Diaper Status	Signal Given/Routine Potty Break

DATE: _____

Potty Time	Poop/Pee/Both	Diaper Status	Signal Given/Routine Potty Break

DATE: _____

Potty Time	Poop/Pee/Both	Diaper Status	Signal Given/Routine Potty Break

Potty Training Journal

_____

_____

_____

_____

_____

_____

_____

_____

_____

_____

_____

_____

_____

_____

_____

_____

_____

_____

_____

_____

_____

_____

_____

_____

_____

_____

_____

_____

_____

_____

_____

_____

_____

_____

_____

_____

_____

_____

_____

_____

_____

_____

_____

_____

_____

_____

_____

_____

_____

_____

_____

_____

_____

_____

_____

_____

_____

_____

_____

_____

_____

_____

_____

_____

_____

_____

_____

_____

_____

_____

_____

_____

_____

_____

_____

_____

_____

_____

_____

_____

_____

_____

_____

_____

_____

_____

_____

_____

_____

_____

_____

_____

_____

_____

_____

_____

_____

_____

_____

_____

_____

_____

_____

_____

_____

_____

_____

_____

_____

_____

_____

_____

_____

_____

_____

_____

_____

_____

_____

_____

_____

_____

_____

_____

_____

_____

_____

_____

_____

_____

_____

_____

_____

_____

_____

_____

_____

_____

_____

_____

_____

_____

_____

_____

_____

_____

_____

_____

_____

_____

_____

_____

_____

_____

_____

_____

_____

_____

_____

_____

_____

_____

_____

_____

_____

_____

_____

_____

_____

POTTY TRAINING "MOMMY & DADDY"

_____

_____

_____

_____

_____

_____

_____

_____

_____

_____

_____

_____

_____

_____

_____

_____

_____

_____

_____

_____

_____

_____

_____

_____

_____

_____

_____

_____

_____

_____

_____

_____

_____

_____

_____

_____

Milestones

Baby's Name:	
Baby's Age:	
Potty Training Journey Start Date:	
Time of Day Best for Training:	
Date & Age of Baby's First Successful Potty Trip:	
Baby's Preferred Potty Signal:	

Steps/Tips that Worked Best for my Child Were:	
Challenges We Faced:	
How We Overcame Those Challenges:	
Time it Took for Baby to Understand the Potty After the Initial Introduction:	
Surprising Things I Learned About My Baby Through Early Potty Training:	

Photo Credit- Regeti's Photography

Photo Credit- Drew Xeron

Photo Credit- Drew Xeron

About the Author

Monique Samuels, a star on Bravo's hit reality television series "The Real Housewives of Potomac," is an entrepreneur, speaker, media personality, writer, and philanthropist. Most importantly, Monique is also a loving wife and mom of three.

She is known for her ability to balance her personal and professional lives and "do it all."

Among her many accomplishments, Monique is the founder of Mila Eve Essentials, an essential products company featuring 100% pure, therapeutic essentials oils and other self care products and CEO of Not For Lazy Moms, a multi-platform media company that provides a destination and online community for resourceful women who want it all and do it all. Not For Lazy Moms began as a blog and has grown into a powerful community where parents can find inspiration for maintaining themselves as well as lifestyle tips and natural alternatives for their families. The website inspired a Not For Lazy Moms podcast, which debuted in August of 2018.

The Not For Lazy Moms community is where people share stories about overcoming obstacles in life, open up about challenges, and share ideas and advice on parenthood, relationships, healthy living, happiness, and so much more.

Monique was born in Atlantic City, New Jersey and graduated from Pleasantville High School as the Salutatorian of her class. She went to Duquesne University to study business law on a full academic scholarship. Monique later decided to put school on hold to pursue a career in music, moved to Washington, DC and worked as an executive assistant for her entertainment attorney in order to pay the bills while she learned more about the music industry.

That was where she met her future husband, former Washington Redskins offensive tackle Chris Samuels, who at the time was looking to start his own record label. Monique and Chris began a great friendship which eventually turned romantic. They dated for six years before they got married in 2012.

Monique and Chris live in Potomac, Maryland with their three children and an African grey parrot, name T'Challa whom Monique is also potty training! You can tune into her podcasts on all major platforms and join the Not For Lazy Moms community at **www.NotForLazyMoms.com** and check out her 100% pure, therapeutic essential oils and other self care products at **www.MilaEveEssentials.com.**

Lightning Source UK Ltd.
Milton Keynes UK
UKHW020100301020
372475UK00006B/82